P9-CCV-148

Sea Otters

Laura Marsh

NATIONAL GEOGRAPHIC

Washington, D.C.

For Quintin, Aidan, Gabriel, and Fiona —L. F. M.

The publisher and author gratefully acknowledge the expert review of this book
by Andrew Johnson, sea otter research and conservation manager
of the Monterey Bay Aquarium.

Paperback ISBN: 978-1-4263-1751-4
Library Edition ISBN: 978-1-4263-1752-1

Book design by YAY! Design

cover, Kevin Schafer/Corbis; 1, Milo Burcham/SuperStock; 2, Blaine Harrington III/Corbis; 4–5, Mark Newman/
Lonely Planet Images/Getty Images; 6 (LO), Tom & Pat Leeson; 6 (UP), Umberto Shtanzman/Shutterstock; 7, Sylvain
Cordier/Hemis.fr RM/Getty Images; 8–9, Francois Gohier/VWPics/Alamy; 10–11, Marvin Dembinsky Photo Associ-
ates/Alamy; 12 (UPLE), altrendo nature/Getty Images; 12 (UPRT), Davies and Starr/The Image Bank/Getty Images;
12 (CTR LE), Colin Keates/Dorling Kindersley/Getty Images; 12 (CTR RT), Datacraft Co Ltd/imagenavi/Getty Images;
12 (LO), Glenn Price/Shutterstock; 13, Bipolar/Taxi/Getty Images; 14, Tom & Pat Leeson; 15, Tom & Pat Leeson;
16, Frans Lanting/Corbis; 17, Howard Hall/SeaPics.com; 18–19, Kerrick James/Corbis; 20 (UP), Tom Soucek/Alaska
Stock; 20 (LOLE), Doc White/naturepl.com; 20 (LORT), IrinaK/Shutterstock; 20–21 (background), Shutterstock;
21 (UPLE), YinYang/E+/Getty Images; 21 (UPRT), Art Wolfe/Science Source; 21 (LO), Morales/age fotostock RM/Getty
Images; 22–23, Alaska Stock/Alamy; 24, Bates Littlehales/National Geographic Creative; 25, Doc White/naturepl
.com; 26–27, Alaska Stock/Alamy; 27 (LO), Marc Moritsch/National Geographic Creative; 28, Randy Wilder/Mon-
terey Bay Aquarium; 29, Natalie B. Fobes/National Geographic Creative; 30 (RT), BMJ/Shutterstock; 30 (LE), Arco
Images GmbH/Alamy; 31 (UPLE), Milo Burcham/SuperStock; 31 (UPRT), Jeff Rotman/Photolibrary RM/Getty Images;
31 (LOLE), Alaska Stock/Alamy; 31 (LORT), Kennan Ward/Corbis; 32 (UPLE), Frans Lanting/Corbis; 32 (UPRT), Jeff
Rotman/Photolibrary RM/Getty Images; 32 (LOLE), TonyV3112/Shutterstock; 32 (LORT), M. Shcherbyna/Shutter-
stock; vocab, Destiny VisPro/Shutterstock

National Geographic supports K–12 educators with ELA Common Core Resources.
Visit natgeoed.org/commoncore for more information.

Printed in the United States of America
15/WOR/2

Table of Contents

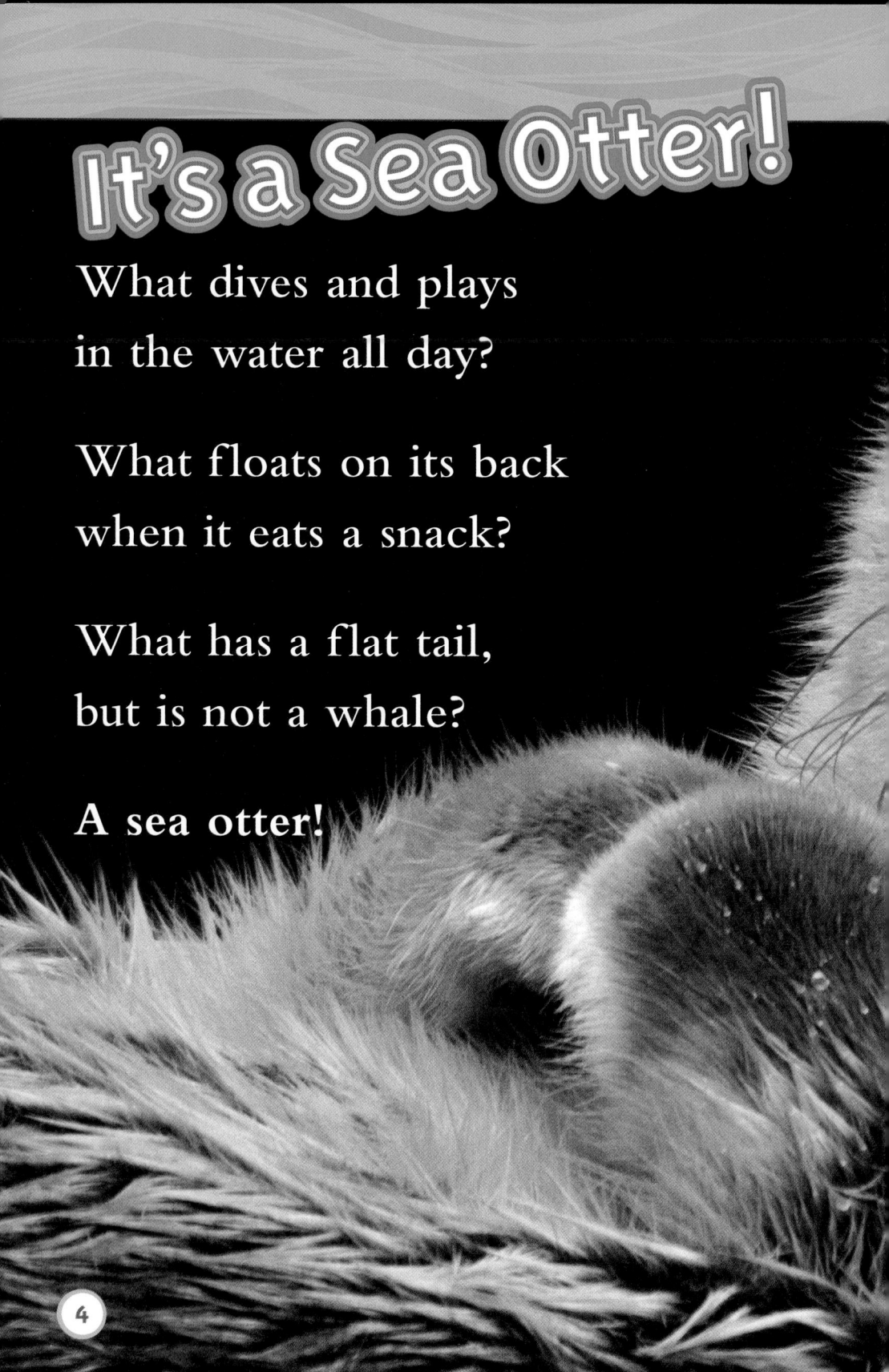

It's a Sea Otter!

What dives and plays
in the water all day?

What floats on its back
when it eats a snack?

What has a flat tail,
but is not a whale?

A sea otter!

What Is a Sea Otter?

Sea otters are mammals. They live in the cold Pacific (puh-SIF-ik) Ocean.

Pacific Ocean

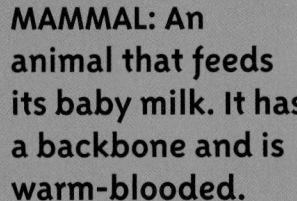

Otter Word

MAMMAL: An animal that feeds its baby milk. It has a backbone and is warm-blooded.

Sometimes sea otters live in zoos or aquariums. They might have been hurt or sick in the wild. Otters get help there.

Otters are fun to watch. They like to play with each other. They dive and splash.

Life in the Sea

Sea otters live close to shore. They find small animals to eat there.

Sea otters dive to the ocean floor. They swim through kelp forests. They need lots of food and clean water to live.

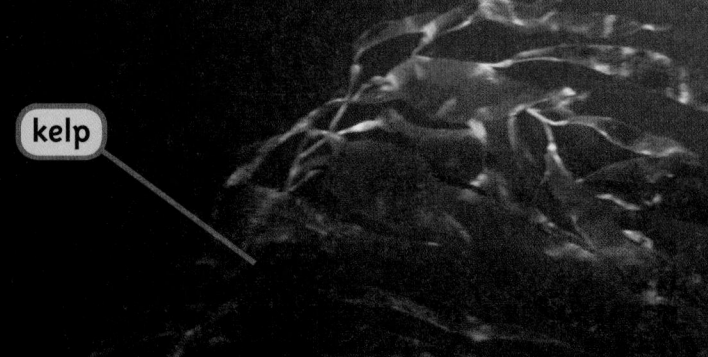

kelp

Q What does an otter say in an emergency?

A Kelp! Kelp!

Otter Word

KELP: A kind of large seaweed that has a long stalk. It can grow into underwater forests.

Built for Hunting

A sea otter's body is perfect for hunting in the water.

TAIL: It helps steer the otter through the water.

BACK LEGS: They are webbed like flippers. They help the otter swim and dive.

FUR: Thick fur keeps the otter warm.

BODY: A long body helps the otter glide through the water.

EYES: Good eyesight helps the otter find food.

NOSTRILS: They close underwater to keep water out.

MOUTH: Sharp teeth tear off bits of food.

FRONT PAWS: They feel and grab for food.

Snack Time

shrimp

scallop

sea urchin

squid

crab

Sea otters eat small animals.
They eat more than 40 different
kinds. They munch on clams, crabs,
squid, urchins, and other animals.
Sea otters have
favorite foods,
just like you.

13

A sea otter cracks open the shell to eat the animal inside.

Sea otters eat their meals above the water. They lie on their backs. They use their stomachs as plates.

But they don't use a knife and fork! Sea otters use rocks to crack open hard shells.

Scrub-a-Dub!

Do you like to stay clean?
Sea otters do.

They groom themselves for hours
every day. They scrub their faces
and bodies with their paws.

They also somersault (SUM-ur-salt), twist, and turn. This washes food scraps off their bodies. Their fur must stay clean to be warm.

Otter Word

GROOM: To clean by scrubbing, licking, or biting

Fuzzy Fur

It's hard to stay warm in cold water. But a sea otter's fur is up to the job. It is thicker than any other animal's fur.

Q What did the teacher say to the otters causing trouble?

A Go on, get otter here!

The fur has two layers. The outside layer keeps the cold water out. The inside layer stays warm and dry.

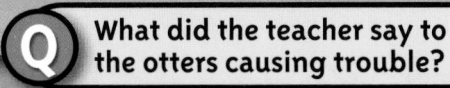

6 Cool Facts About Sea Otters

1 Sometimes sea otters hold hands (well, paws)!

2 Sea otters can hold their breath for about five minutes. Most people can't do this for more than one minute.

3 They are members of the weasel family.

4

They eat ten pounds or more of food each day. This gives them energy to swim and hunt.

5

They are the smallest sea mammals in the world.

6

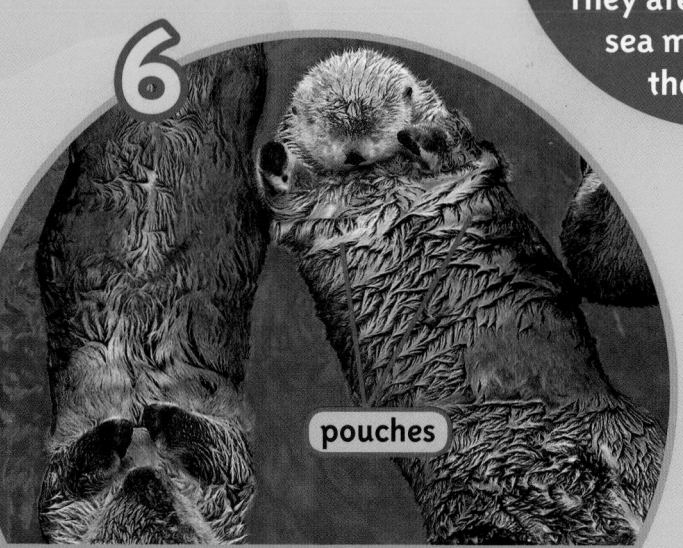

pouches

Sea otters have their own pockets. They put food in a pouch under each front leg while hunting.

Playful Pups

A mother otter often floats with her pup on her chest.

Q What is an otter's favorite book series?

A Harry Otter!

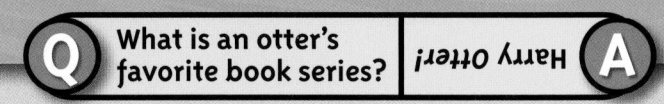

Baby sea otters are born in the water. They are called pups.

Pups are about two feet long at birth. That's about as long as two cereal boxes.

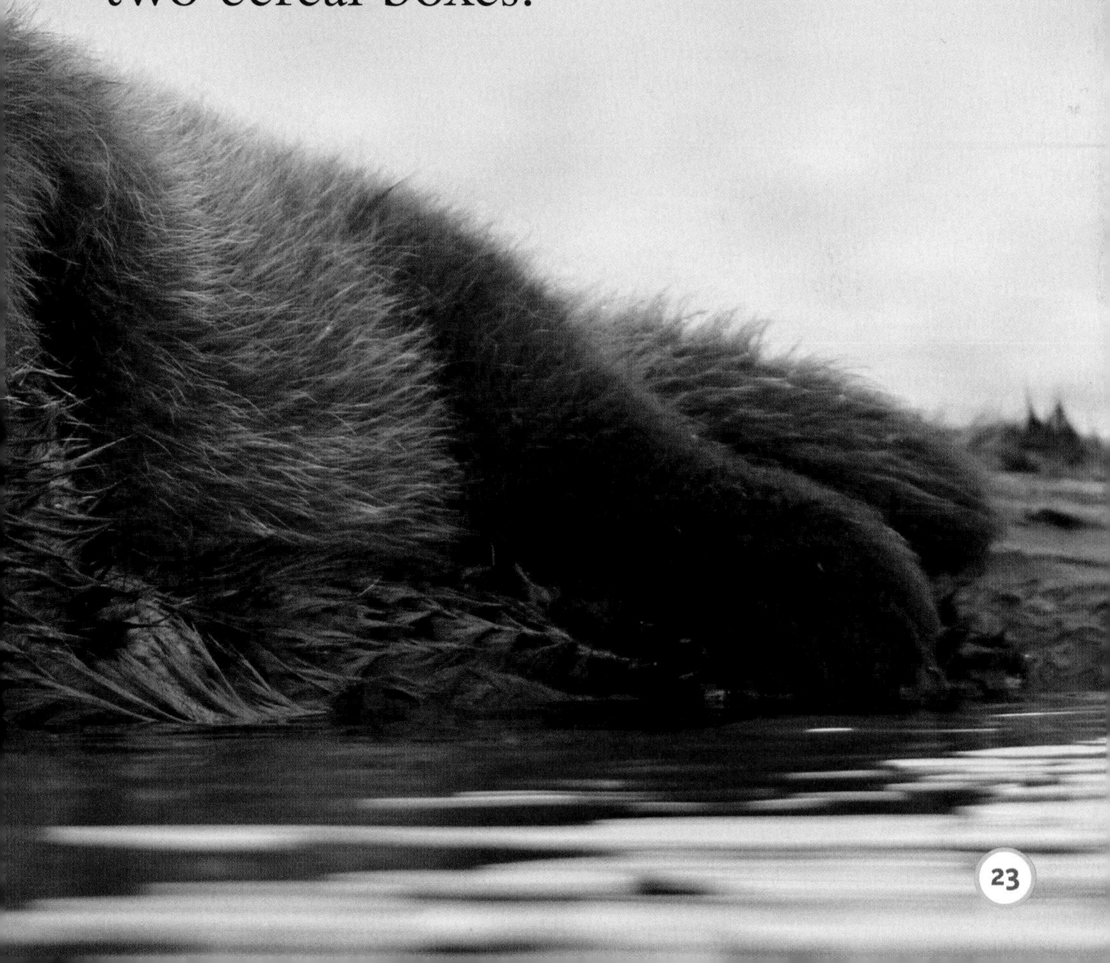

The mother teaches
her pup how to swim,
dive, and roll. But she
does the hunting until
the pup is older.

A mother may wrap her pup in kelp when she dives. Then the pup will stay in one place while she is away.

Taking It Easy

Sea otters live in groups called rafts. The groups are usually all boys or all girls. They spend lots of time together. They rest, groom, and eat.

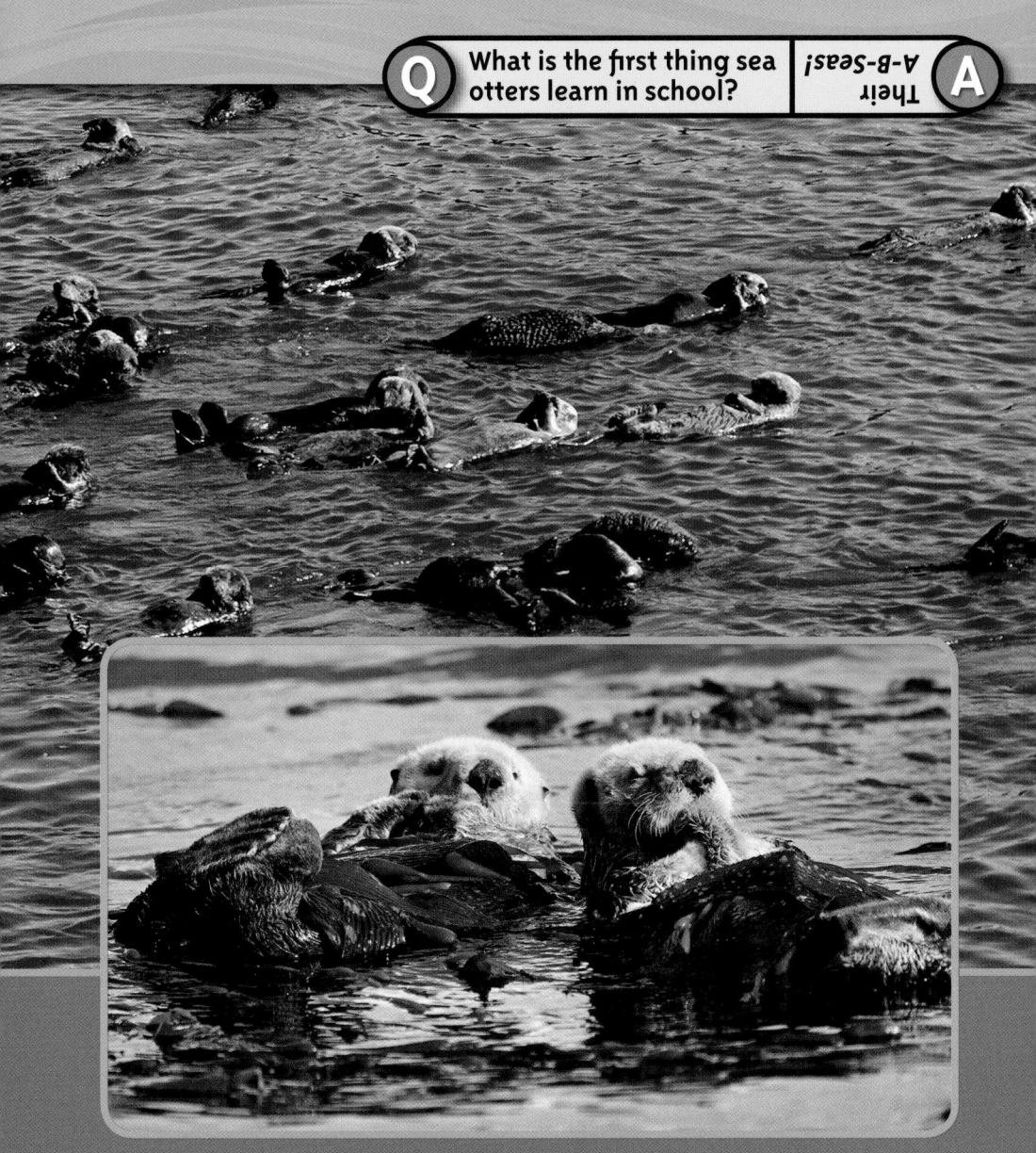

Q What is the first thing sea otters learn in school?

A Their A-B-Seas!

Otters in rafts often wrap themselves in kelp, too. They may sleep like this, side by side.

27

Watching Out for Otters

Scientists are busy studying sea otters. They want to know how otters live and eat. They want to learn about otters that have gotten sick or hurt, too. Then they can help.

A scientist weighs a sea otter at the Monterey Bay Aquarium.

Scientists do know that pollution (pol-LOO-shun) hurts sea otters. Keeping pollution out of the ocean helps sea otters stay healthy.

Otter Word

POLLUTION:
Dangerous material that makes the water, air, or soil dirty

This sea otter was rescued from an oil spill. People helped clean and care for it.

What in the World?

These pictures show close-up views of sea otter things. Use the hints below to figure out what's in the pictures. Answers on page 31.

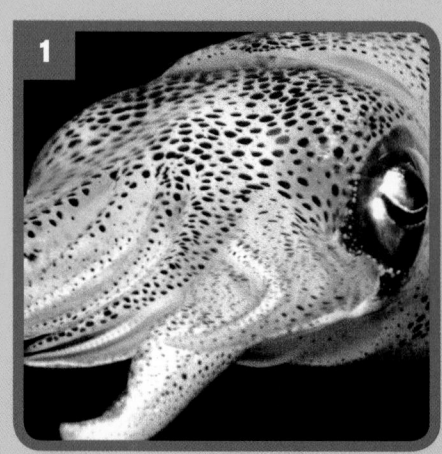

HINT: An animal that sea otters like to eat

HINT: Sea otters live here.

WORD BANK

kelp	teeth	paws	squid	fur	ocean

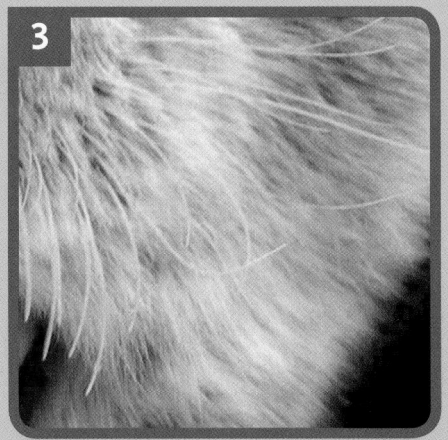

HINT: This keeps otters warm in cold water.

HINT: A kind of tall seaweed

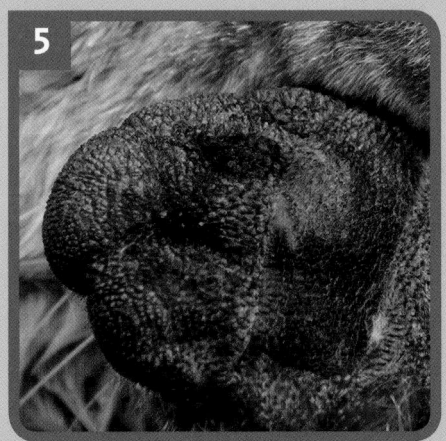

HINT: These are used to grab food.

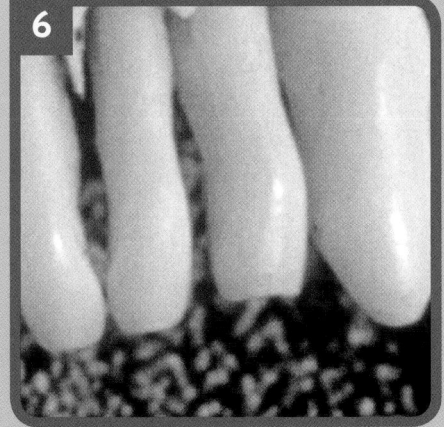

HINT: They tear off bits of food.

Answers: 1. squid, 2. ocean, 3. fur, 4. kelp, 5. paws, 6. teeth

GROOM: To clean by scrubbing, licking, or biting

KELP: A kind of large seaweed that has a long stalk. It can grow into underwater forests.

MAMMAL: An animal that feeds its baby milk. It has a backbone and is warm-blooded.

POLLUTION: Dangerous material that makes the water, air, or soil dirty

Manatees

Laura Marsh

NATIONAL GEOGRAPHIC

Washington, D.C.

For Paul —L. F. M.

The publisher and author gratefully acknowledge the expert review
of this book by Deborah Epperson, Ph.D.

Trade paperback ISBN: 978-1-4263-1472-8
Reinforced library binding ISBN: 978-1-4263-1473-5

Book design by YAY! Design

Photo Credits

Cover, Brian J. Skerry/National Geographic Creative; 1, Masa Ushioda/SuperStock; 2, Luis Javier Sandoval/Oxford Scientific/Getty Images; 4–5, Alex Mustard/naturepl.com; 6, SuperStock; 8 (UP), Mike Kemp/Rubberball/Corbis; 8 (LO), Millard H. Sharp/Science Source; 9, Digital Vision/Getty Images; 10 (UP), Wayne Lynch/All Canada Photos/Corbis; 10 (LE), Visuals Unlimited/Getty Images; 10 (LO), Helmut Corneliimageb/SuperStock; 11, David Fleetham/Visuals Unlimited/Getty Images; 12, Dave Fleetham/Design Pics/Corbis; 14, Fred Bavendam/Minden Pictures; 15, Tom Brakefield/Purestock/SuperStock; 16 (UPLE), Jeff Foott/Discovery Channel Images/Getty Images; 16 (UPRT), Lonely Planet Images/Getty Images; 16 (LO), Mauricio Handler/National Geographic Creative; 16-17 (Background), tristan tan/Shutterstock; 17 (UPLE), Jurgen Freund/naturepl.com; 17 (UP CTR), Pat Canova/Alamy; 17 (UPRT), Dorling Kindersley/Getty Images; 17 (LOLE), Franco Banfi/WaterFrame RM/Getty Images; 17 (LORT), Wayne Lynch/All Canada Photos/Getty Images; 18, Richard Olsenius/National Geographic Creative; 19, SFP/Getty Images; 20-21, Daniel J. Cox/Corbis; 22—23, Carl Mehler and Sven M. Dolling; 24, St. Petersburg Times/Vragovic, Will/ZUMA Press/Corbis; 26, Biosphoto/SuperStock; 26 (INSET), Jeff Foott/Discovery Channel Images/Getty Images; 27, Jurgen Freund/naturepl.com; 29, NHPA/SuperStock; 30 (UP), Greg Amptman/Shutterstock; 30 (CTR), Greg Amptman/Shutterstock; 30 (LO), Mauricio Handler/National Geographic Creative; 31 (UPLE), Greg Amptman/Shutterstock; 31 (UPRT), Greg Amptman/Shutterstock; 31 (CTR), Wayne Johnson/Shutterstock; 31 (LO), Dave Fleetham/Design Pics/Corbis; 32 (UPLE), Alex Mustard/naturepl.com; 32 (UPRT), Fred Bavendam/Minden Pictures; 32 (CTR LE), Thorsten Milse/Robert Harding World Imagery/Getty Images; 32 (CTR RT), Paul Looyen/Shutterstock; 32 (LORT), NHPA/SuperStock; Water Words header, Lonely/Shutterstock; vocab, Memo Angeles/Shutterstock

Table of Contents

Who Am I?

I have whiskers,
but I am not a cat.

I nibble on grass,
but I am not a cow.

I have gray, wrinkled skin, but I am not an elephant.

Who am I?
A manatee!

Mighty Manatees

Manatees often rest in groups.

Manatees are mammals that live in the water. They are sometimes called "sea cows."

Why?

Manatees are gentle and they move slowly, like cows. They also graze on sea grass, just like cows eat grass.

Water Words

MAMMAL: An animal that has a backbone and is warm-blooded. It feeds its babies milk.

GRAZE: To feed in an area covered with grasses

Manatees are big. They are usually about ten feet long. That's as long as two kids' bikes lined up end to end.

Manatees are heavy, too.
Most adult manatees weigh about
1,000 pounds. That's the weight
of about 21 second graders!

Super Swimmers

Manatees can move their large bodies gracefully through the water. They swim upside down and roll. They even do somersaults (SUM-ur-sawlts)!

A group of manatees swims in Crystal River, Florida, U.S.A.

Manatees don't like water that is too deep. They like to stay in shallow water in oceans and rivers. There, they find food and warm water.

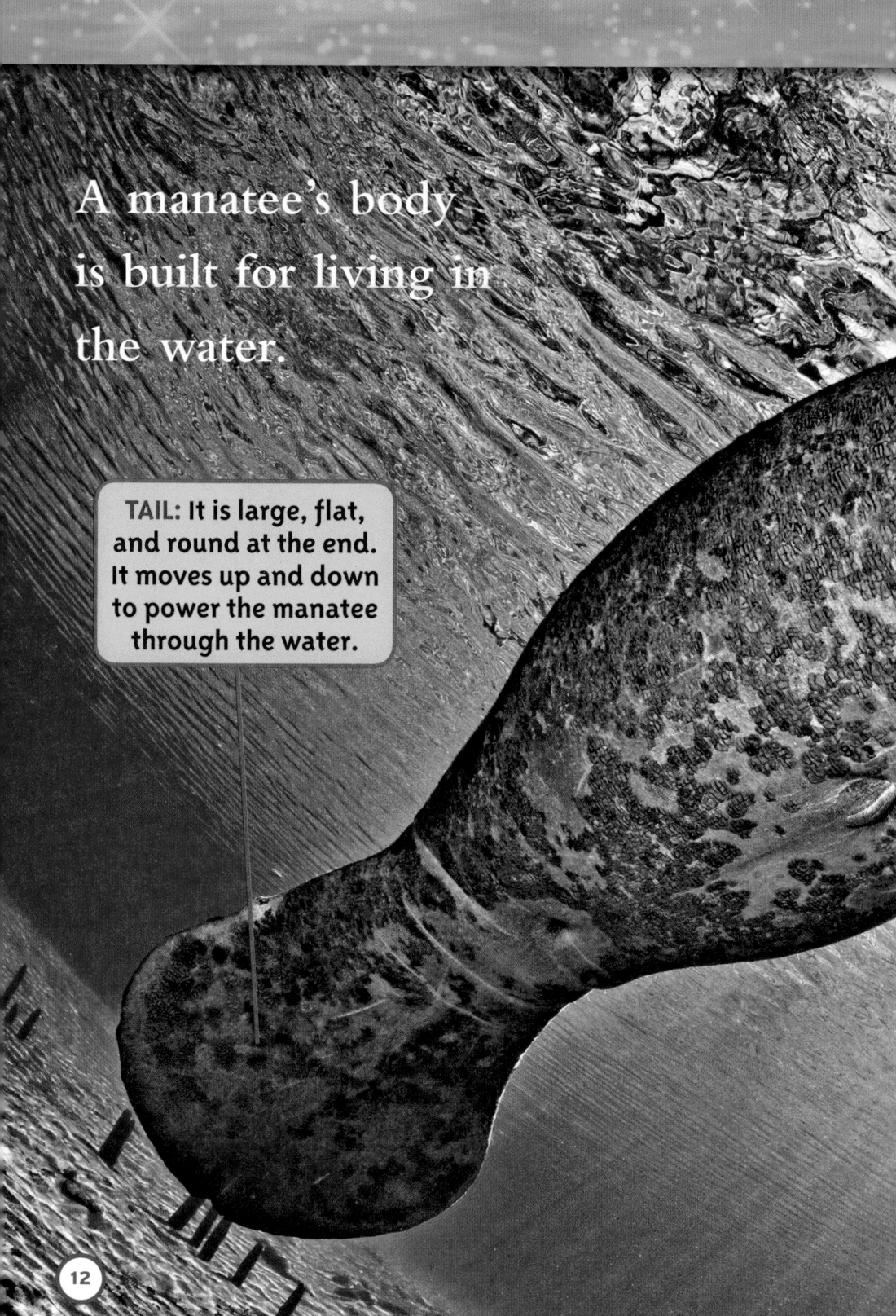

A manatee's body
is built for living in
the water.

TAIL: It is large, flat, and round at the end. It moves up and down to power the manatee through the water.

EYES: They are small, but manatees can see well, even in cloudy water.

NOSTRILS: Manatees breathe air through these holes. But they close tightly underwater.

FLIPPERS: They help steer the manatee. They also bring food to its mouth.

LIPS: They are big and strong. They wrap around plants and pull them into the manatee's mouth.

Munching on Lunch

Manatees are herbivores (HUR-buh-vores). They eat plants for about six to eight hours every day.

A manatee grazes on sea plants.

Manatees have no front teeth.
They don't need them because
they don't eat meat.

Manatees have only large back teeth
called molars. The molars help
grind their food.

Water
Word

HERBIVORE: An animal
that eats only plants

15

7 Fun Facts About Manatees

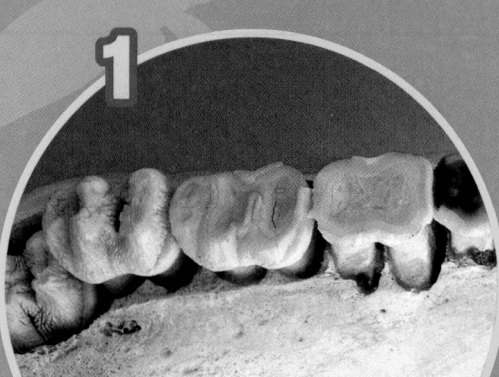

1

They lose teeth all through their lives. New teeth replace them.

2

The elephant is a distant relative of the manatee.

3

Fat in the mother's milk helps a young manatee grow quickly.

4 They do not have eyelashes.

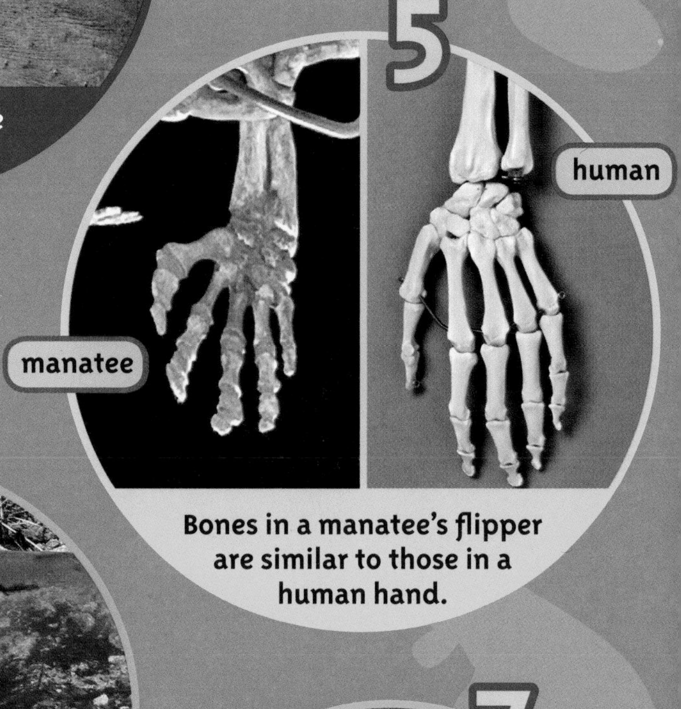

5

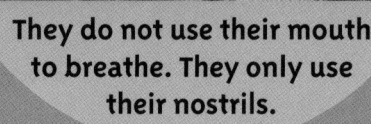 manatee

human

Bones in a manatee's flipper are similar to those in a human hand.

6 They do not use their mouth to breathe. They only use their nostrils.

7

They have no natural enemies. Humans are their biggest threat.

Big Babies

These young manatees are fed milk from a bottle. Without their mothers, they need help to eat.

A manatee baby is called a calf. It is born underwater. A newborn calf is about the size of a nine-year-old kid.

The mother pushes the calf to the surface to take its first breath. Within an hour, the calf can swim on its own.

Like other mammal babies, a manatee drinks its mother's milk. Soon it learns how to find sea grasses to eat.

A calf needs to stick with its mom.

Q What do manatees learn in school?

A Their A-B-Seas!

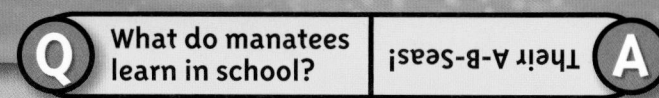

The calf must stay with its mother for the first two years. The mother teaches her calf how to live on its own.

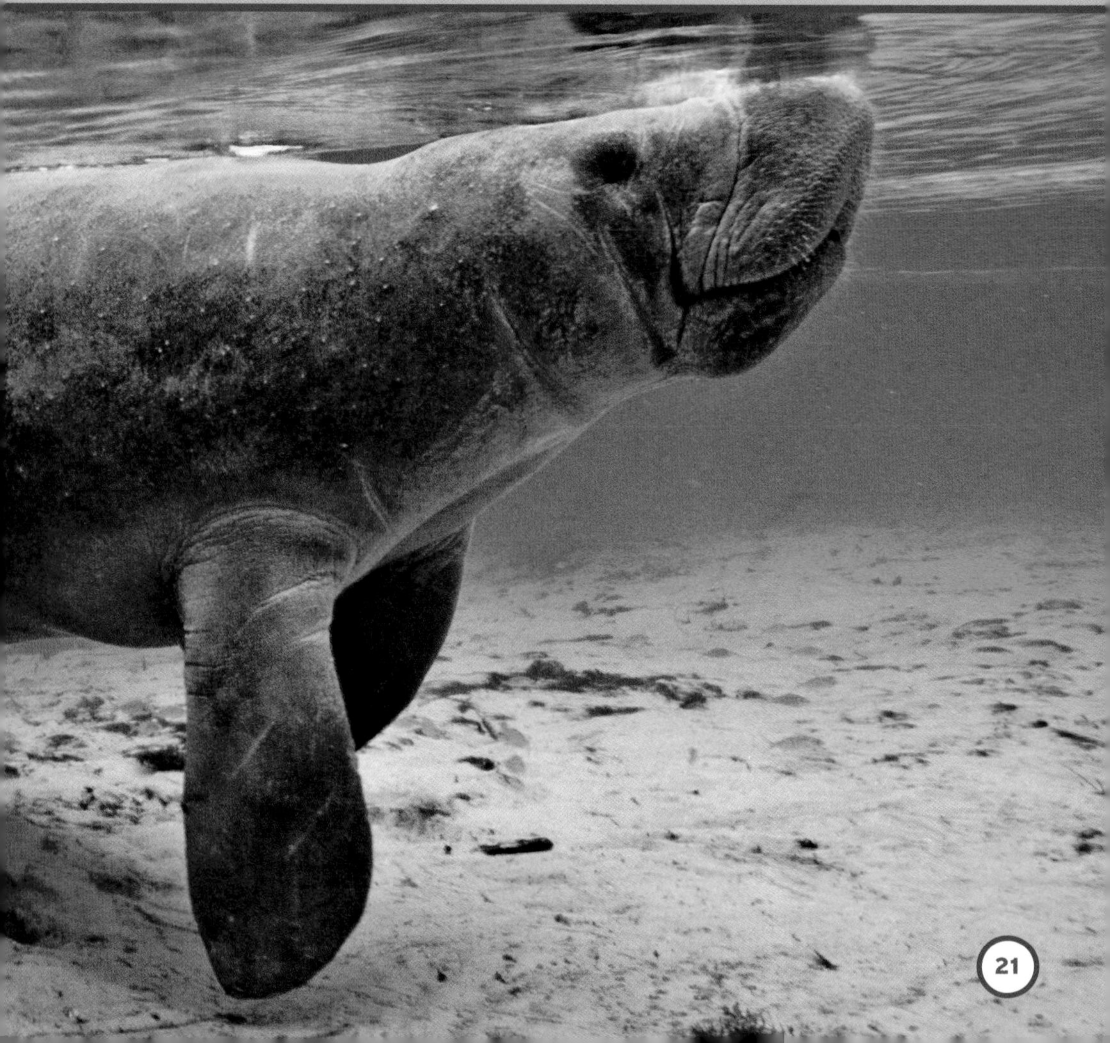

On the Move

Manatees do not stay in one place. They migrate (MY-grate).

In summer, manatees can be found in many states. In winter, most manatees return to Florida. The water is warmer there.

Water Word

MIGRATE: To move from one area to another for food or a mate

North America

UNITED STATES

FLORIDA

TEXAS

U

S

Area where Florida manatees live year-round

Area where Florida manatees travel in summer

MILES
0   200   400

KILOMETERS
0   200   400

CANADA

UNITED
STATES

MISSISSIPPI

LOUISIANA

ALABAMA

GEORGIA

SOUTH
CAROLINA

NORTH CAROLINA

VIRGINIA

MARYLAND

Chesapeake Bay

FLORIDA

ATLANTIC OCEAN

BAHAMAS

Florida Keys
Straits of Florida

GULF OF MEXICO

23

Manatees at Rest

Manatees don't usually travel in groups. But they often rest together in warm water.

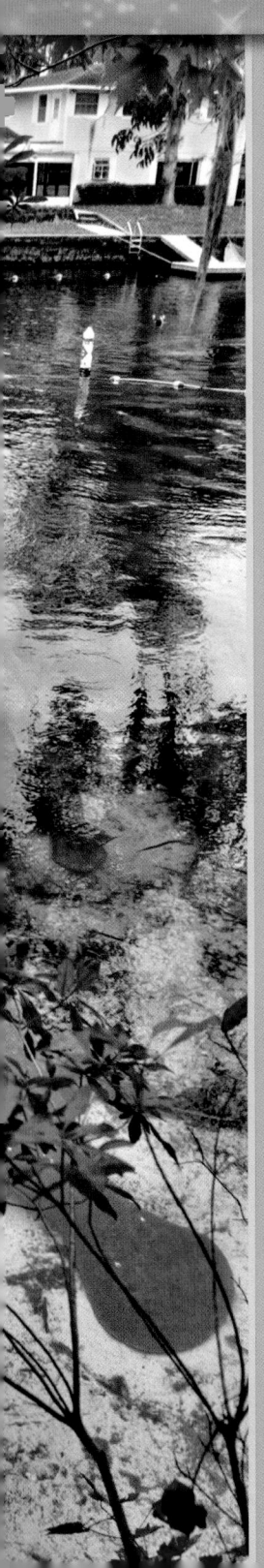

Manatees need rest, like you. But they don't sleep like you do.

They rest for about 15 minutes at a time. Then they need to come to the surface to breathe.

Manatees sometimes rest at the bottom of the sea or river. They can also float near the top of the water when resting.

Keeping Manatees Safe

There are many dangers for manatees. They are often hit by boats because they are big and slow and swim near the surface. Manatees can be hard to see in the water.

Manatee Zone
SLOW SPEED
MINIMUM WAKE
Sep 1 - Apr 30
35 MPH Day 25MPH Night
May 1 - Aug 31

This manatee has scars from an injury by a boat propeller.

People also throw trash and fishing line into the water. Swallowing trash can hurt manatees. Fishing line can get tangled around manatees so they can't swim.

Manatees are endangered
(in-DANE-jurd).
There are about 5,000
Florida manatees left.

But laws protect them.
There are also special
areas for manatees called
sanctuaries (SANGK-choo-
er-eez). In a sanctuary,
people can't disturb
manatees. They can live
safely there and raise
their young.

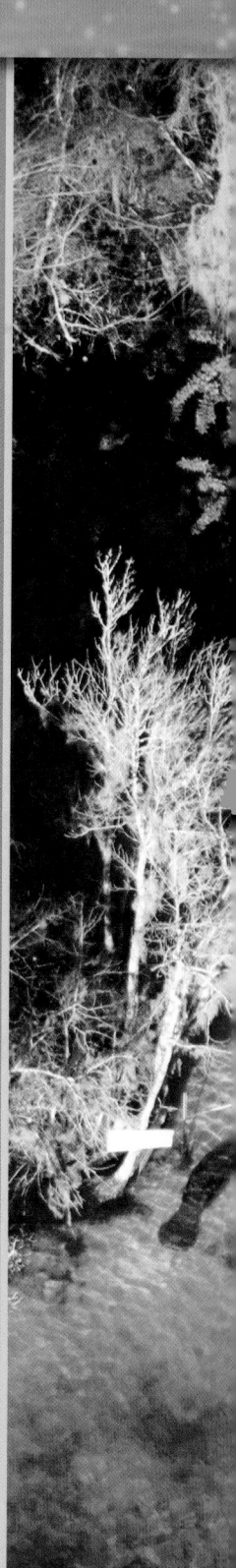

The roped-off area shows where people are not allowed to go.

Water Word

ENDANGERED: At risk of dying out

SANCTUARY: A safe place set aside for animals in nature

Stump Your Parents

Can your parents answer these questions about manatees? You might know more than they do!

Answers at bottom of page 31.

1

Where do manatees live?
A. In cool, refreshing water
B. In warm, shallow water
C. In deep, warm water
D. On the beach

2

A baby manatee is called . . .
A. A cub
B. A cow
C. A calf
D. A foal

3

What do manatees like to eat?
A. Plants
B. Crabs
C. Fruit
D. Steak

4

A manatee's lips . . .

A. Are very small
B. Are perfect for lipstick
C. Get in the way when eating
D. Grab and pull plants into its mouth

5

Manatees rest . . .

A. For many hours
B. For about 30 minutes at a time
C. For about 15 minutes at a time
D. Not at all

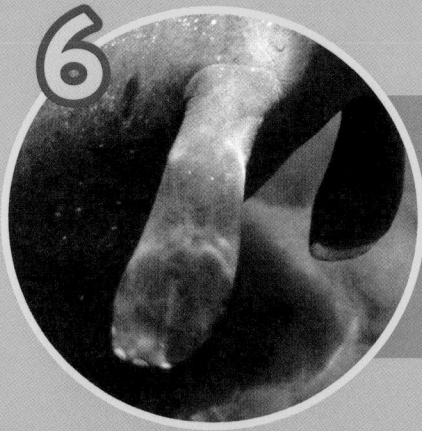

6

A manatee uses its flippers to . . .

A. Do the backstroke
B. Slap the water
C. Steer through the water
D. Wave to other manatees

7

To keep manatees safe, people should NOT . . .

A. Bother manatees in any way
B. Drive boats really fast
C. Throw trash in the water
D. Do any of the above

Answers: 1) B, 2) C, 3) A, 4) D, 5) C, 6) C, 7) D

ENDANGERED: At risk of dying out

GRAZE: To feed in an area covered with grasses

HERBIVORE: An animal that eats only plants

MAMMAL: An animal that has a backbone and is warm-blooded. It feeds its babies milk.

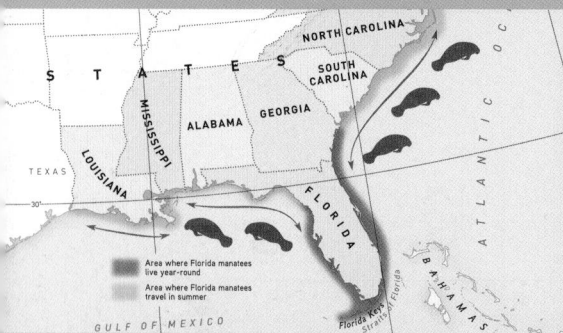

MIGRATE: To move from one area to another for food or a mate

SANCTUARY: A safe place set aside for animals in nature

LEVEL 2

Sea Turtles

Laura Marsh

NATIONAL GEOGRAPHIC

Washington, D.C.

For Eliza

—L. F. M.

Design by Yay Design

Paperback ISBN: 978-1-4263-0853-6
Hardcover ISBN: 978-1-4263-0854-3

National Geographic supports K—12 educators with ELA Common Core Resources.
Visit natgeoed.org/commoncore for more information.

Table of Contents

A Sea Turtle!

Green sea turtle

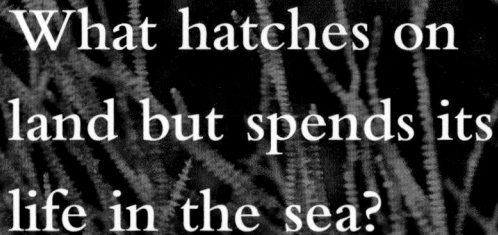

What hatches on land but spends its life in the sea?

What starts out the size of a Ping-Pong ball but can grow up to seven feet long?

A sea turtle!

Ocean World

Leatherback sea turtle

Sea turtles are graceful swimmers in the water. Their flippers move like wings.

Turtle Term

REPTILE: A cold-blooded animal that lays eggs and has a backbone and scaly skin

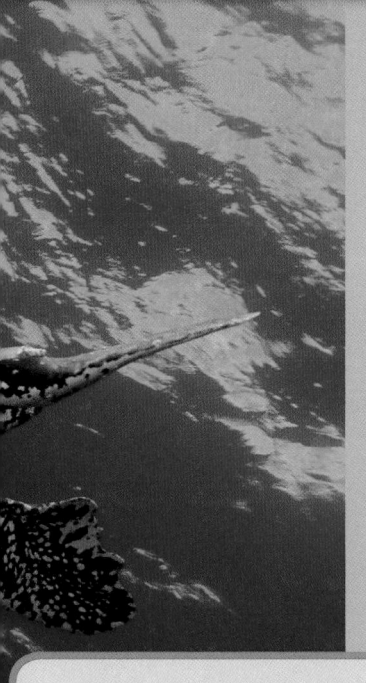

Sea turtles travel the world in warm ocean waters. They are one of the few reptiles that live in the sea.

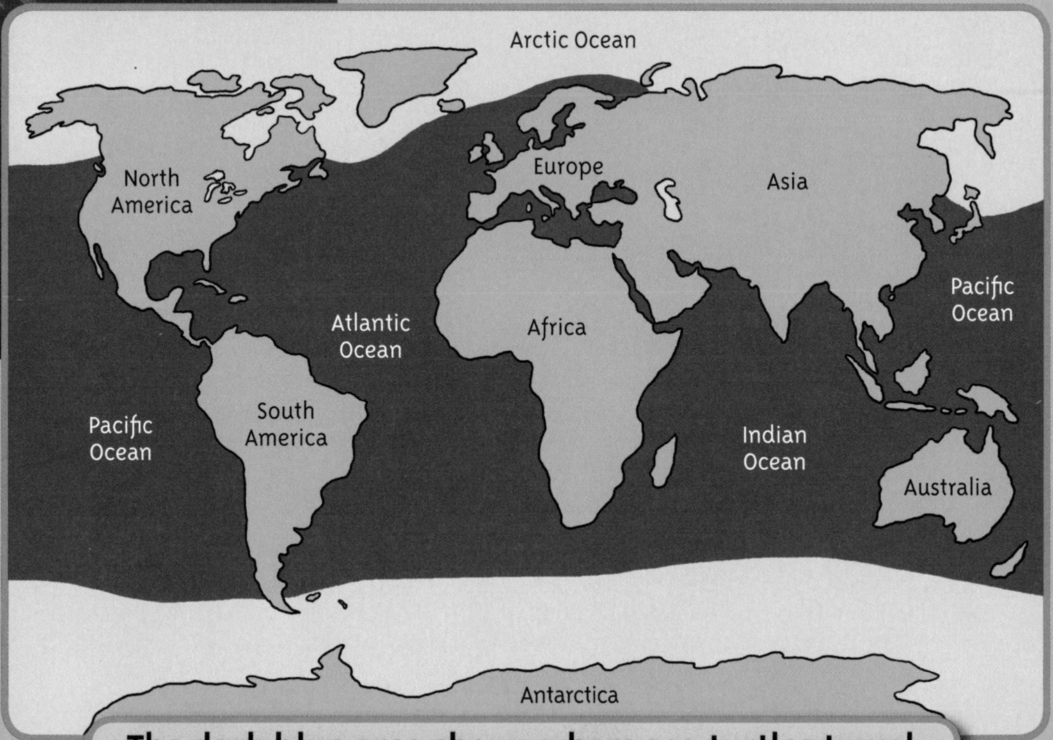

Arctic Ocean

North America

Europe

Asia

Pacific Ocean

Atlantic Ocean

Africa

Pacific Ocean

South America

Indian Ocean

Australia

Antarctica

The dark blue area shows where sea turtles travel.

A sleek body helps
the turtle move easily
through the water.

The scales
on its shell are
called scutes.

The back flippers steer
the turtle as it swims.
They are also used to
dig nests in the sand.

Green sea turtle

A sea turtle has lungs because it breathes air. A sea turtle holds its breath underwater.

Sea turtles can't pull their heads and limbs into their shells like land turtles can.

Their large, powerful flippers act like paddles.

Scientists believe some sea turtles live 80 years or more, but they don't know for sure.

Meet the Turtles!

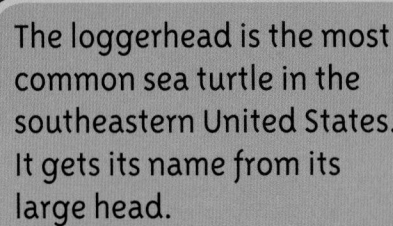

The loggerhead is the most common sea turtle in the southeastern United States. It gets its name from its large head.

There are seven kinds of sea turtles in the world. Each has special features.

The flatback has a flat body. It's the only sea turtle that doesn't live in U.S. waters. It lives near Australia.

The olive ridley has an olive-colored shell. It is shaped like a heart.

The hawksbill can't dive deep. It spends most of its time on the water's surface.

The green turtle has a small head. Unlike other sea turtles, it goes ashore to warm itself in the sun.

The Kemp's ridley likes shallow waters. It's the world's most endangered sea turtle.

Turtle Term

ENDANGERED: At risk of dying out

The leatherback doesn't have a hard shell. Its skin is rubbery with small bones underneath.

Nestbuilding

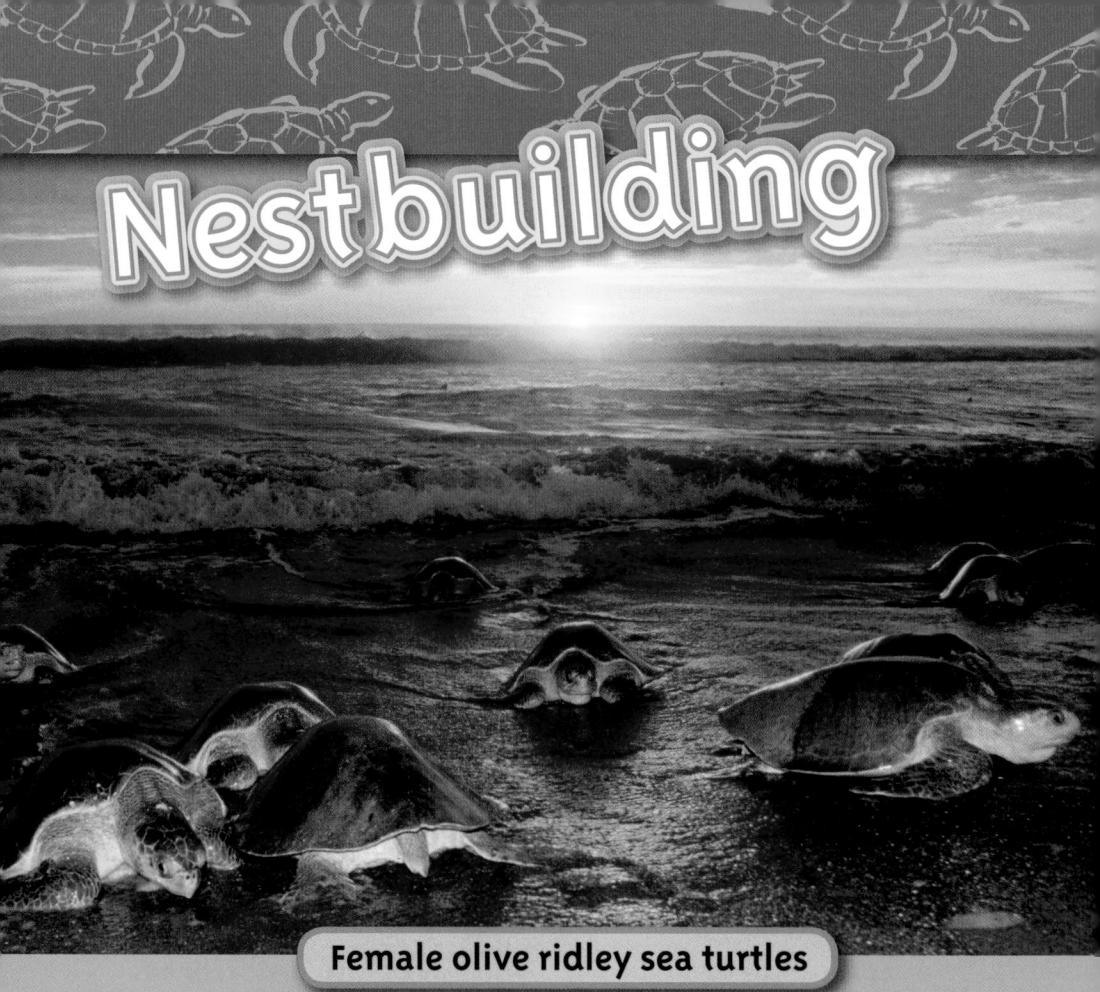

Female olive ridley sea turtles

A female sea turtle comes on land to lay her eggs. She usually returns to the same beach where she hatched.

Scientists aren't sure how sea turtles know where to go. They think sea turtles know by instinct.

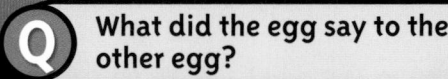
The sea turtle digs a hole with her back flippers. She lays her eggs and covers them with sand. Then she returns to the sea.

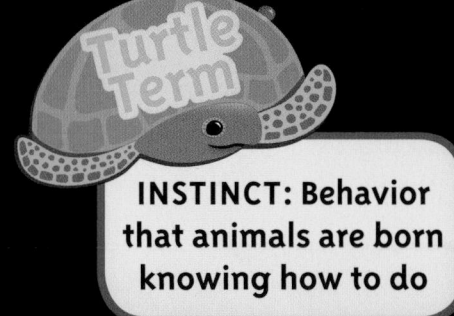

Turtle Term

INSTINCT: Behavior that animals are born knowing how to do

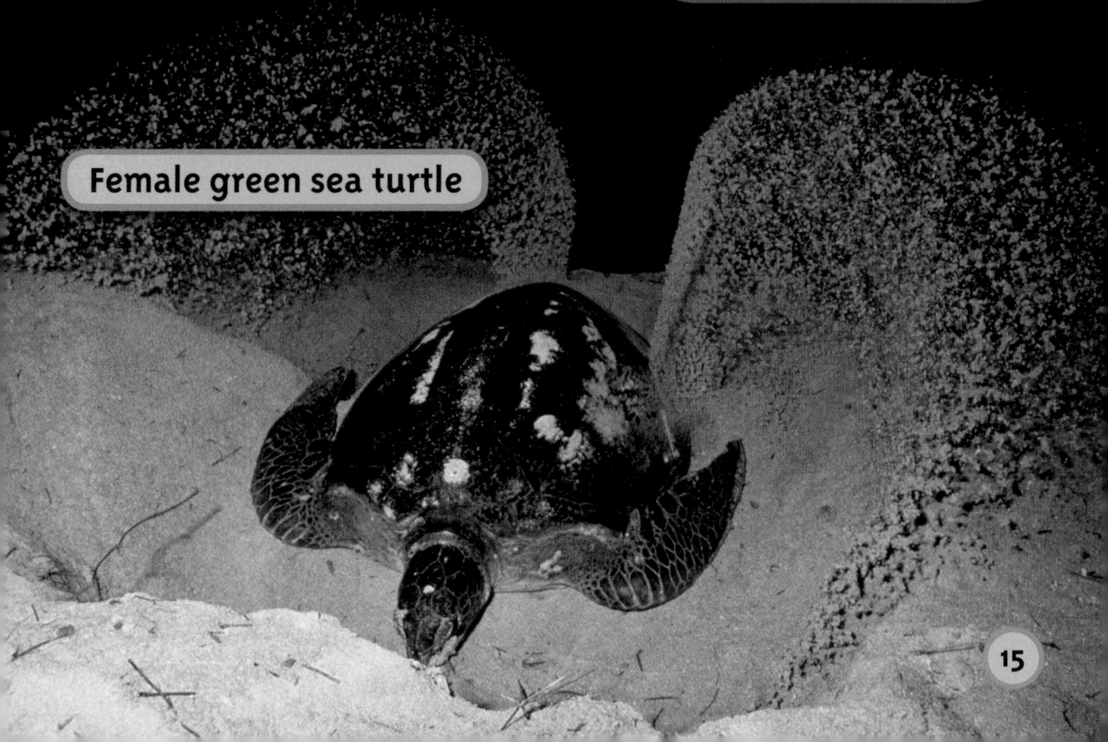

Female green sea turtle

15

Oh, Baby!

CRAAACK! The eggs hatch after 50 to 70 days. Tiny turtles called hatchlings crawl out of their eggshells.

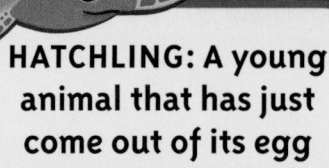

Turtle Term

HATCHLING: A young animal that has just come out of its egg

They are less than
three inches long.

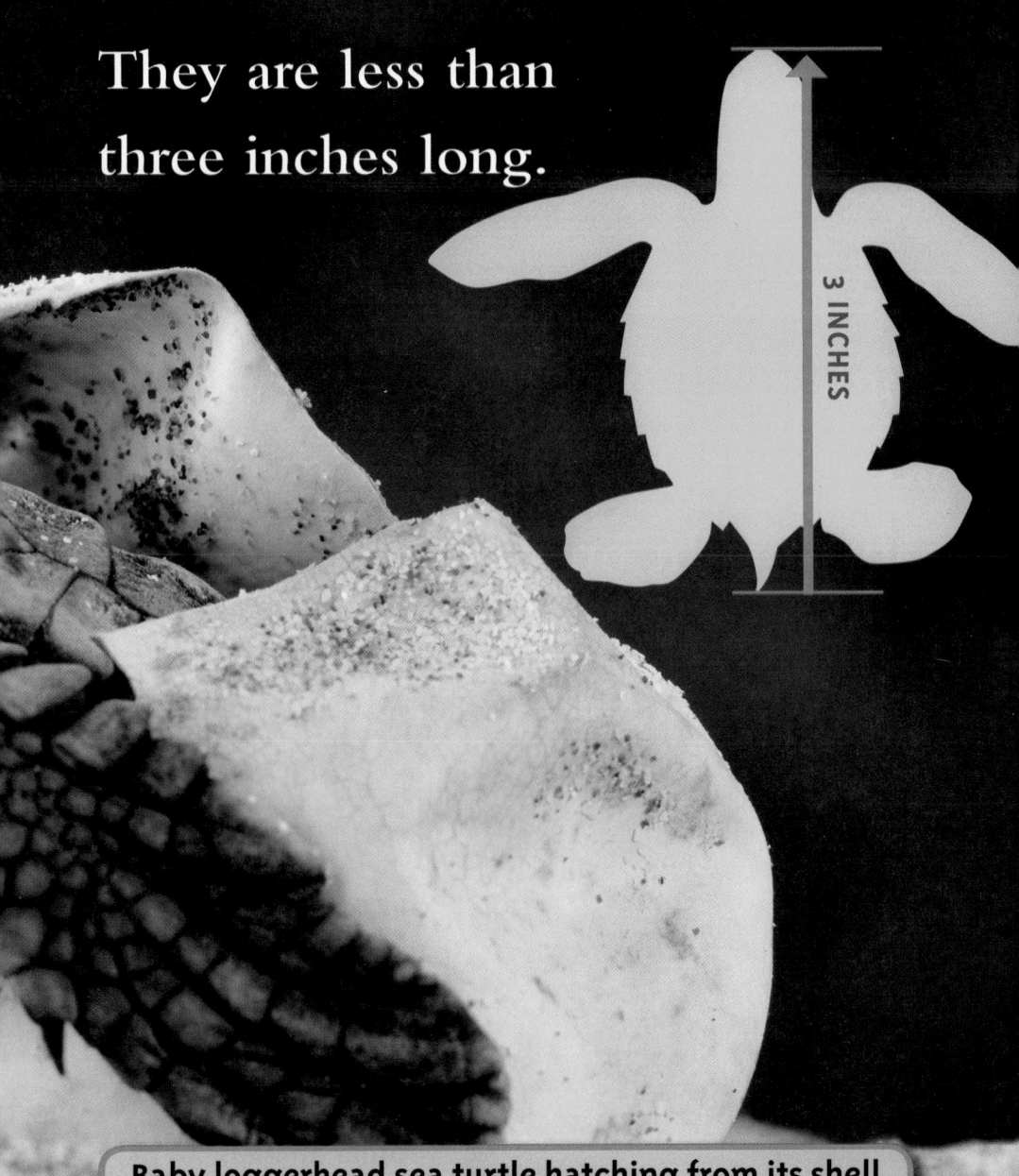

3 INCHES

Baby loggerhead sea turtle hatching from its shell

Hatchlings usually crawl toward the sea at night. In the dark, they are hidden from predators.

The little turtles follow the brightest light. The line where the sky meets the sea is the brightest natural light on a beach.

If the hatchlings follow this light, they will make it to the sea.

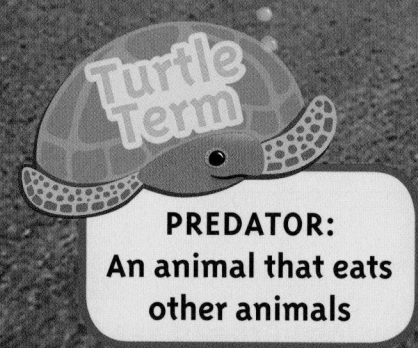

Turtle Term

PREDATOR:
An animal that eats other animals

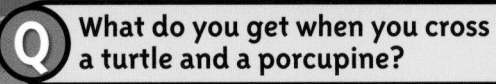

Q What do you get when you cross a turtle and a porcupine?

A A slowpoke!

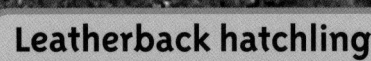

Leatherback hatchling

Big and Small

The smallest sea turtles are the Kemp's ridley and the olive ridley. Adults are about two feet long and weigh up to 100 pounds.

Kemp's ridley sea turtle

Leatherback sea turtle

The largest sea turtle is the Leatherback. It can grow up to seven feet long and weigh more than 2,000 pounds. That's about ten men put together!

On the Menu

Green sea turtle

Munch, munch, what's for lunch?

Most sea turtles eat plants and animals. They dine on algae (AL-gee) and sea grasses. They also munch on crab and conchs.

Turtle Term

ALGAE: Simple, non-flowering plants that do not have stems, roots, or leaves

Jellyfish are a favorite food for many sea turtles. But plastic trash can look like jellyfish in the ocean, and that spells trouble! Swallowing trash can hurt and even kill sea turtles.

Green sea turtle

Danger!

Hawksbill sea turtle caught in a net

Trash isn't the only danger to sea turtles. Fishing nets and hungry animals can harm them, too.

Building lights confuse hatchlings so they don't reach the sea.

Leatherback sea turtle confused by city lights

Sometimes people even step on sea turtle nests by accident.

Sea Turtle Rescue

In 2010 a giant oil spill leaked into the Gulf of Mexico. Oil covered sea animals and washed up on beaches. Oil is dangerous to people and wildlife.

Oil on beaches in Louisiana

Oil-covered Kemp's ridley

27

People in charge of a sea turtle rescue program in Louisiana saved many sea turtles.

The rescuers cleaned the turtles and gave them medicine. People cared for them until they could return to the sea.

Kemp's ridley sea turtle

Safekeeping

You don't need to work at a sea turtle hospital to help sea turtles. Here are a few things you can do to keep them safe.

1

Pick up trash on the beach.

2

Don't release balloons into the air. (They often end up in the sea.)

3

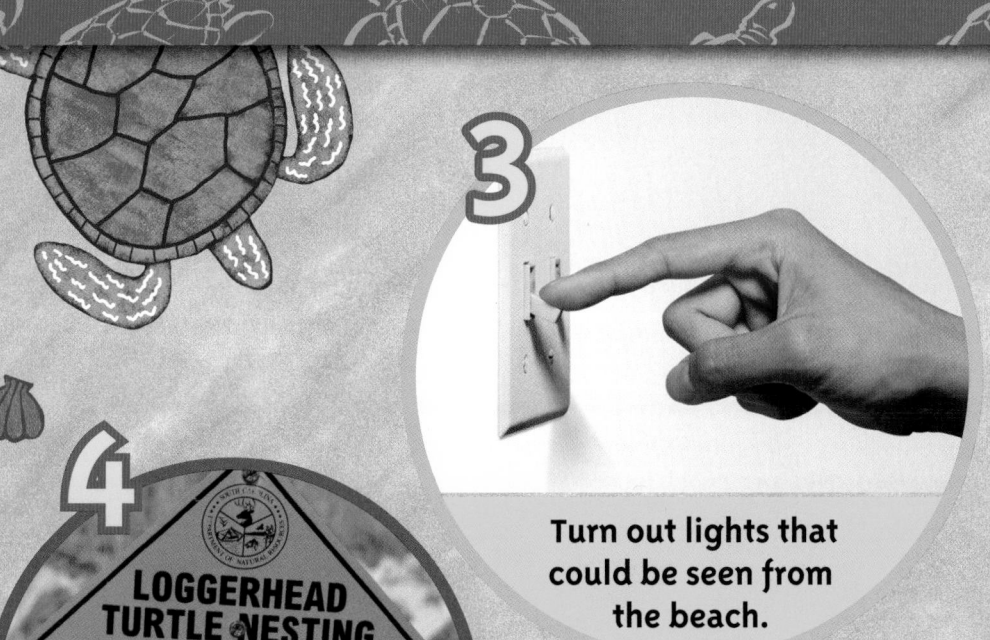

Turn out lights that could be seen from the beach.

4

LOGGERHEAD TURTLE NESTING AREA

Eggs, Hatchlings, Adults, and Carcasses are Protected By Federal & State Laws

Contact
1-800-922-5431
www.dnr.sc.gov/seaturtle/

Read beach warning signs. Avoid turtle nesting areas.

5

Tell your classmates what you've learned about sea turtles.

Glossary

ALGAE: Simple, non-flowering plants that do not have stems, roots, or leaves

ENDANGERED: At risk of dying out

HATCHLING: A young animal that has just come out of its egg

INSTINCT: Behavior that animals are born knowing how to do

PREDATOR: An animal that eats other animals

REPTILE: A cold-blooded animal that lays eggs and has a backbone and scaly skin

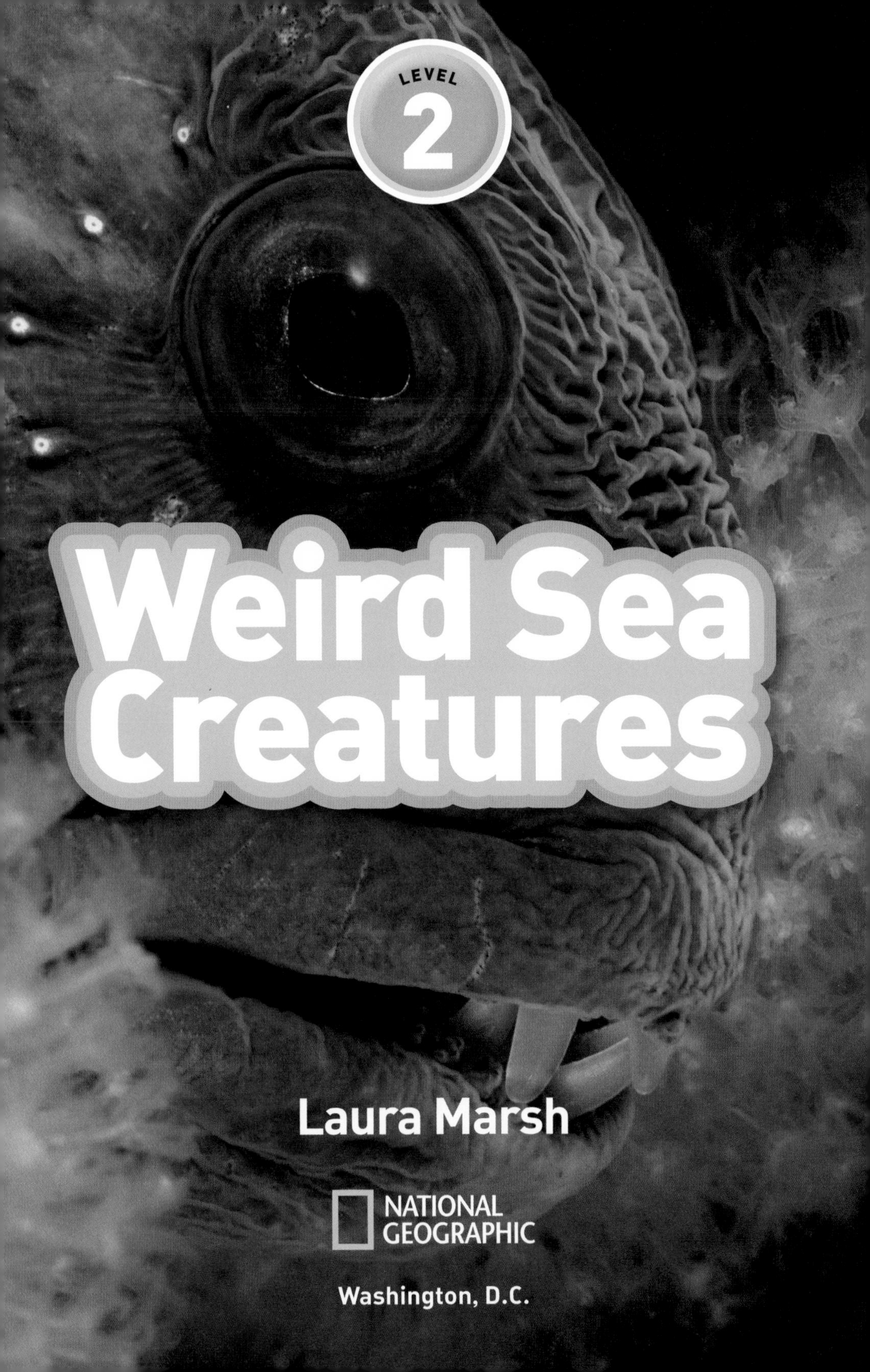

LEVEL 2

Weird Sea Creatures

Laura Marsh

NATIONAL GEOGRAPHIC

Washington, D.C.

For Finn and Zoë
—L. F. M.

National Geographic gratefully acknowledges the assistance of the National Aquarium.

This material is based upon work supported by the National Science Foundation under Grant No. DRL-1114251. Any opinions, findings, and conclusions or recommendations expressed in this material are those of the author(s) and do not necessarily reflect the views of the National Science Foundation.

As seen on the National Geographic Channel

Design by YAY! Design

Paperback ISBN: 978-1-4263-1047-8
Library edition ISBN: 978-1-4263-1048-5

Photo credits

Table of Contents

Strange But True

balloonfish

Many strange sea creatures live in the ocean.

Some are beautiful. Some are ugly. Some are cute, and some are scary.

Weird sea creatures are strange for a reason. The funny way they look and the strange things they do help them live in the ocean.

Survival Skills

Snorkeling in shallow water

diagonal butterflyfish

Some sea animals live in the shallow ocean waters. Some live in the deep ocean.

The ocean can be a hard place to live. Deep areas are cold and dark. It can be hard to find food.

And the ocean can be dangerous. There are many predators. Any animal can quickly become dinner for another animal.

Water Word

PREDATOR: An animal that hunts and eats other animals

Sea creatures have special skills that help them find food. They also have strange body parts that can help them hide and stay safe from other animals.

How weird are these sea creatures? Let's find out!

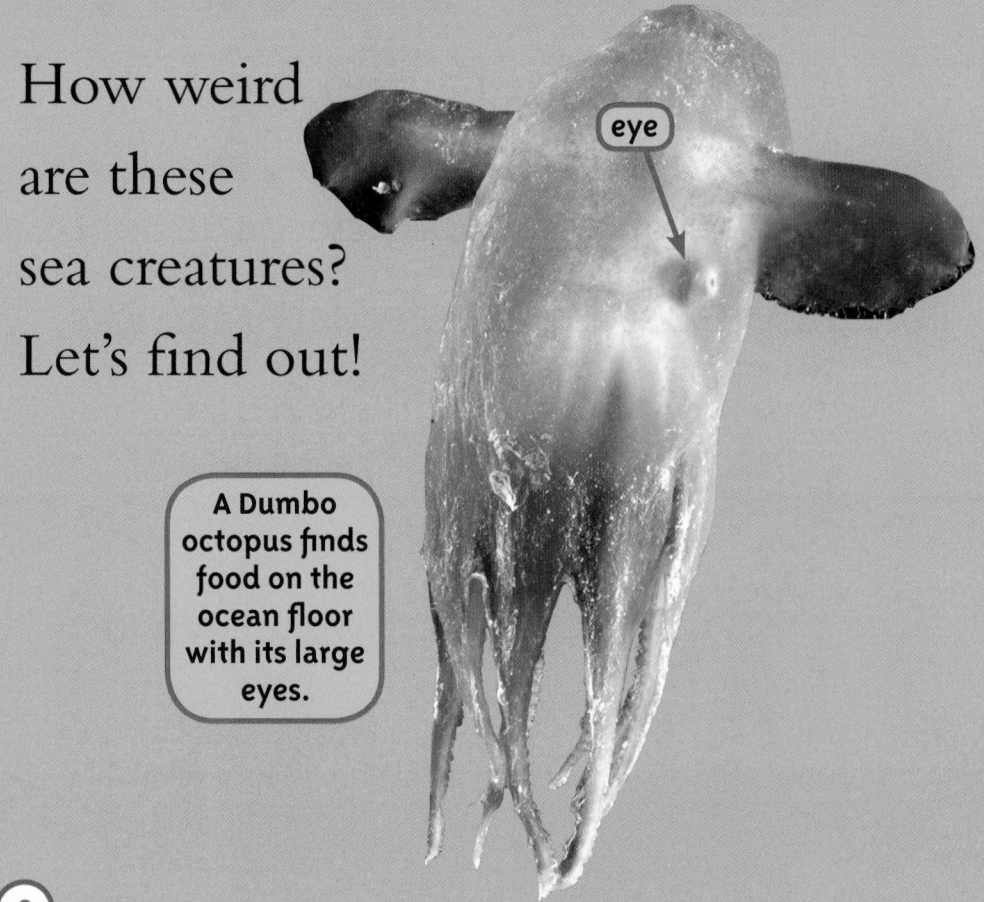

eye

A Dumbo octopus finds food on the ocean floor with its large eyes.

A leafy sea dragon blends in with the seaweed around it.

A moray eel's sharp teeth catch prey.

Hide and Seek

Camouflage (KAM-uh-flazh) helps animals hide from their enemies. Looking strange helps them blend in to the plants or water around them.

Camouflage also helps animals catch dinner. Do you see the stonefish in the picture? Most fish don't because it looks like rock or coral. When they swim too close, the stonefish springs from the ocean floor. It grabs dinner in a flash.

Water Word
CAMOUFLAGE: An animal's natural color or form that blends in with what is around it

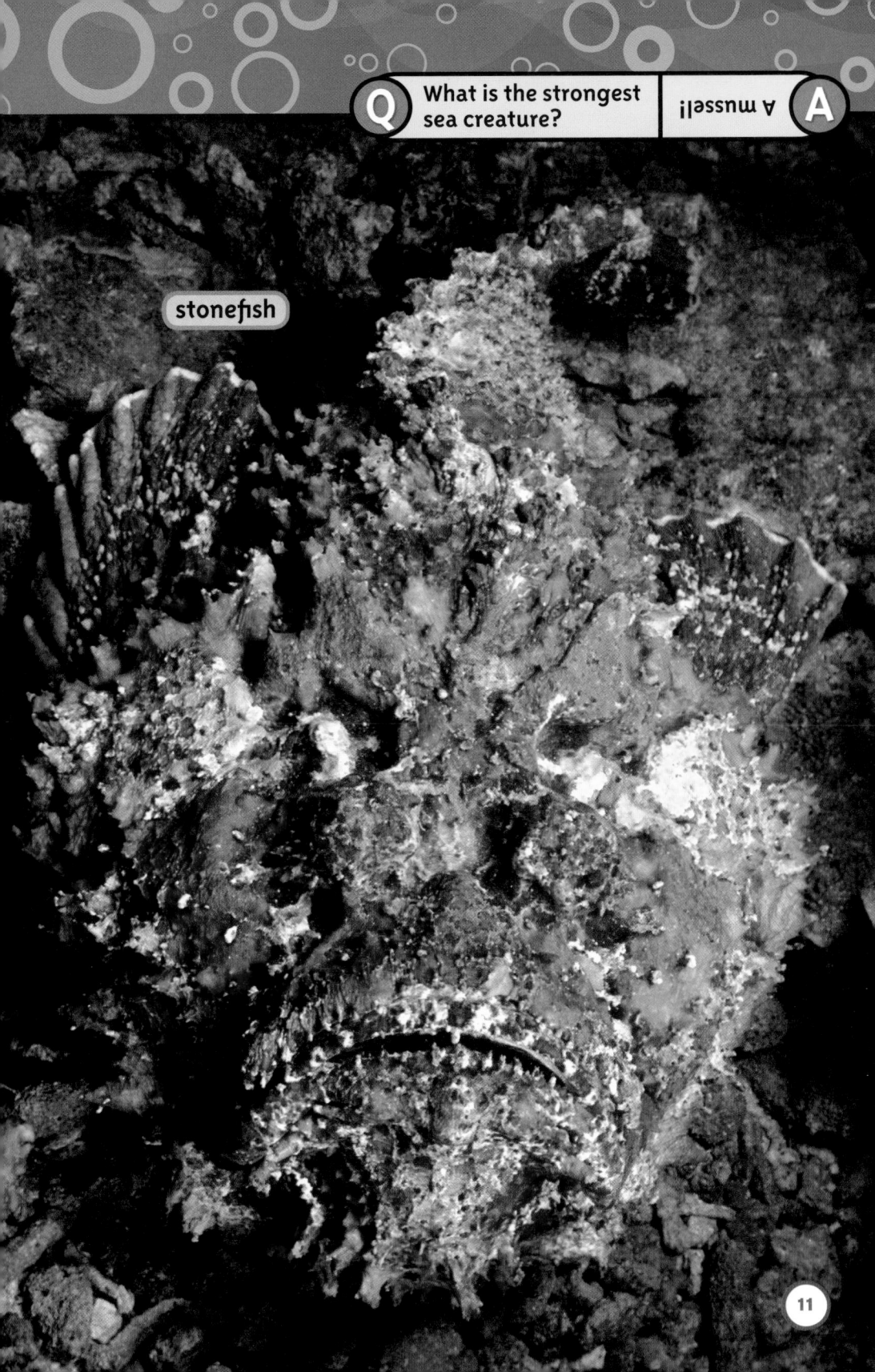

stonefish

11

Big Eyes

The deep ocean gets very little light. Many animals that live there have large eyes. Big eyes help creatures see in the darkness and find prey.

viperfish

hatchetfish

This viperfish used its big eyes to spot a hatchetfish. Dinnertime!

The hatchetfish uses its own large eyes to find tiny shrimp to eat in the dark sea.

Water Word

PREY: An animal that is eaten by another animal

Making Light

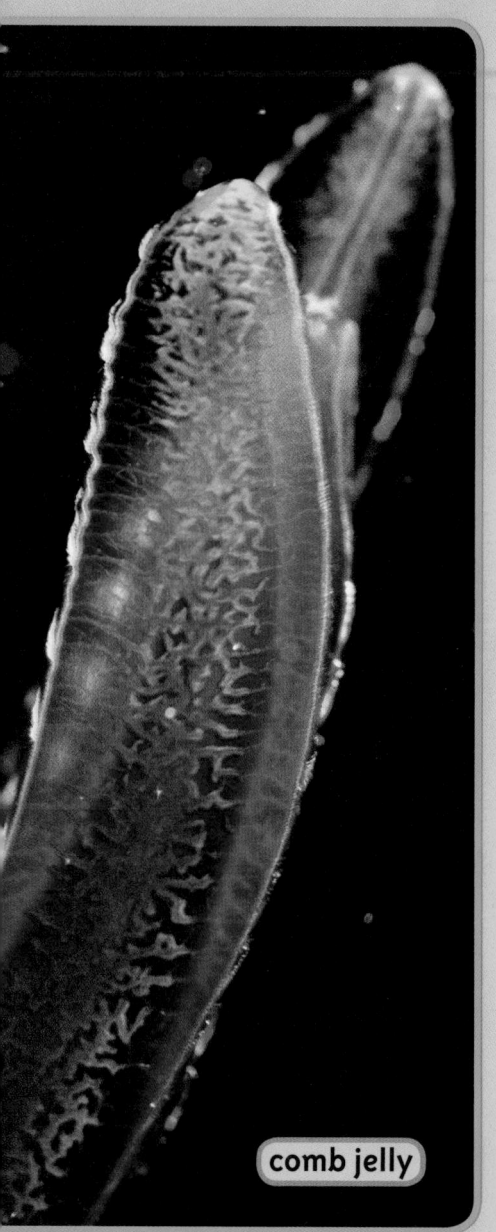

comb jelly

Many creatures in the deep, dark sea have a special trick—they make their own light! This is called bioluminescence (BYE-oh-loom-i-NESS-ants).

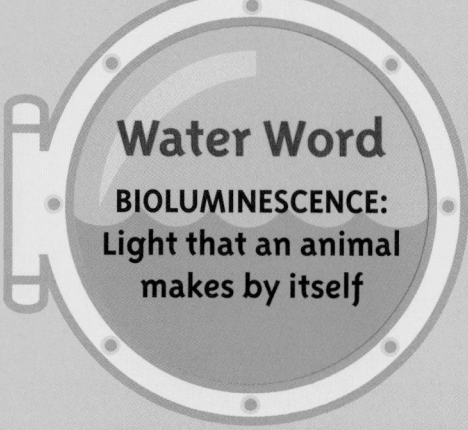

Water Word
BIOLUMINESCENCE: Light that an animal makes by itself

Some sea creatures use their own light as a flashlight to find prey. Light can draw prey toward an animal, too. And light can surprise enemies, so an animal can make a quick escape.

patch that glows

Expert Food Finders

Some animals have wacky body parts that help them catch meals.

mouth

gulper eel

The gulper eel has a super-long tail. Prey comes closer for a better look. This eel's giant mouth opens wide. It can eat an animal bigger than it is. It can't be picky. In the deep sea, the eel must eat whatever it can find.

tail

The tiny cookie-cutter shark locks onto its prey with strange sucking lips. Its sharp teeth sink in. They leave a bite the shape of a circle.

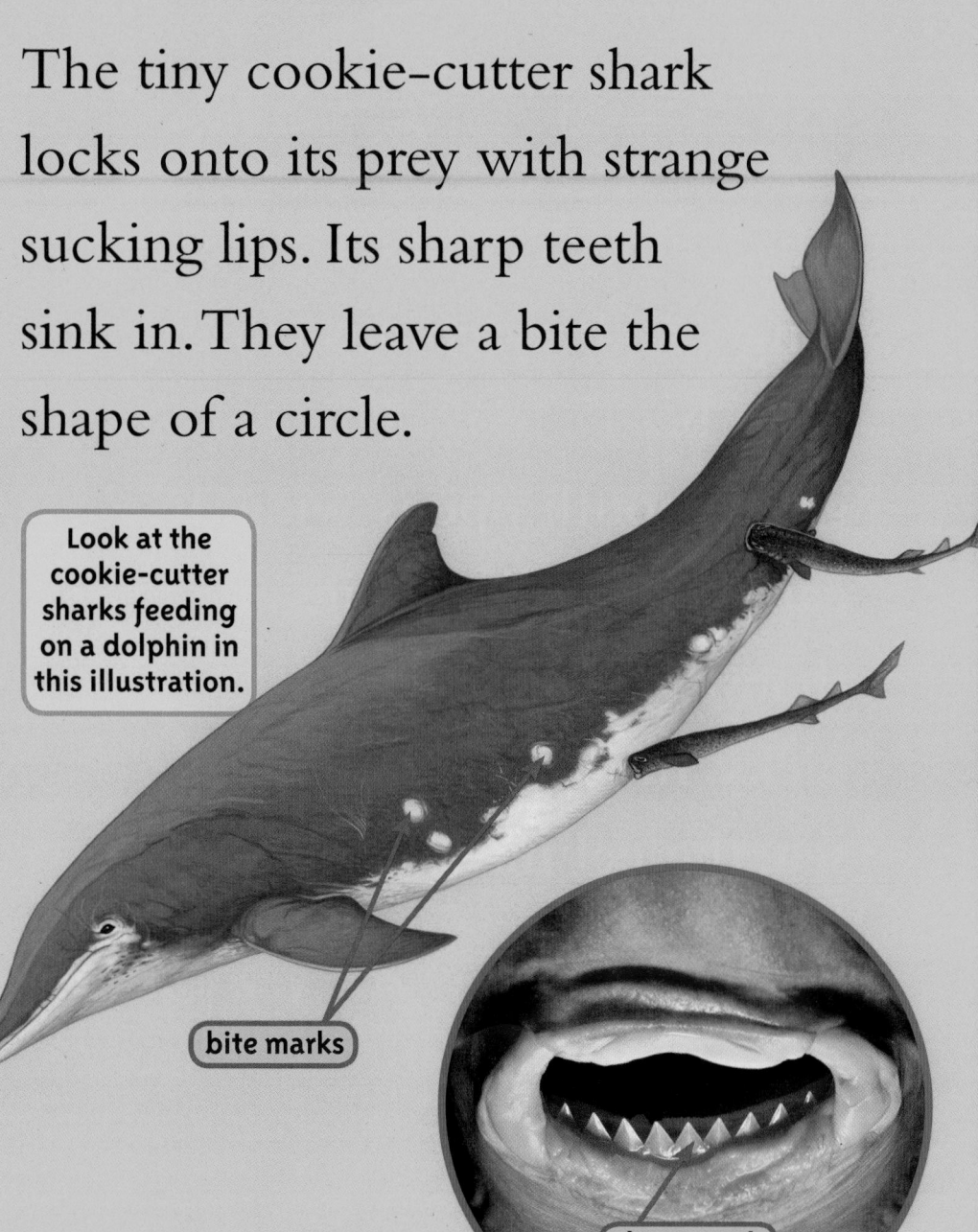

Look at the cookie-cutter sharks feeding on a dolphin in this illustration.

bite marks

sharp teeth

fishing lure

anglerfish

An anglerfish has its own fishing pole called a lure. The lure glows, and other fish want to know what it is. When they get close, the anglerfish eats them.

Deadly Dangers

Bumping into some sea creatures can be bad news.

The yellow sea anemone (ah-NEM-oh-nee) looks like a pretty flower. But it has stinging parts that have deadly venom. When a fish is stung, its muscles stop working. Then the anemone eats the fish.

yellow sea anemone

Water Word

VENOM: A liquid some animals make that can cause stinging, pain, or death

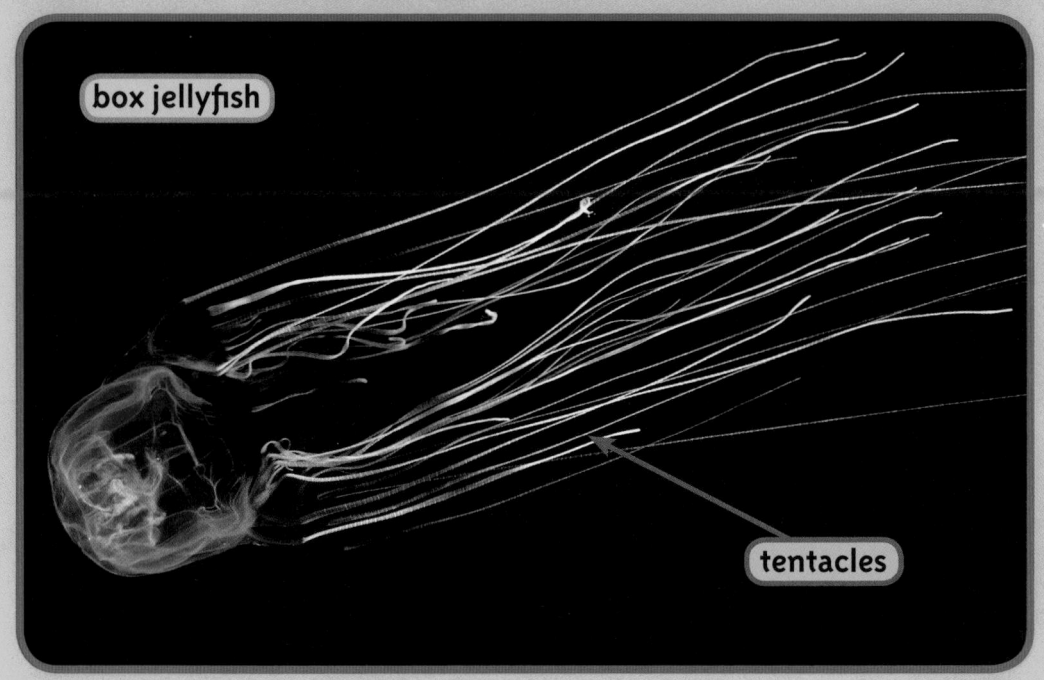

box jellyfish

tentacles

The box jellyfish is one of the most dangerous animals in the world. It has arms called tentacles (TEN-tah-kullz) that grow up to ten feet long. The tentacles deliver a painful, deadly sting.

This lionfish has crazy spiky fins. But you wouldn't want to touch them. The fins on its back are sharp and can sting you.

fins with venom

lionfish

23

Strange Senses

Some animals near the ocean floor don't even have eyes! They can't see their food. So they use other senses to find it.

A sea cucumber can feel tiny pieces of food stuck to its tube feet. It curls its feet in and licks them clean.

sea cucumber

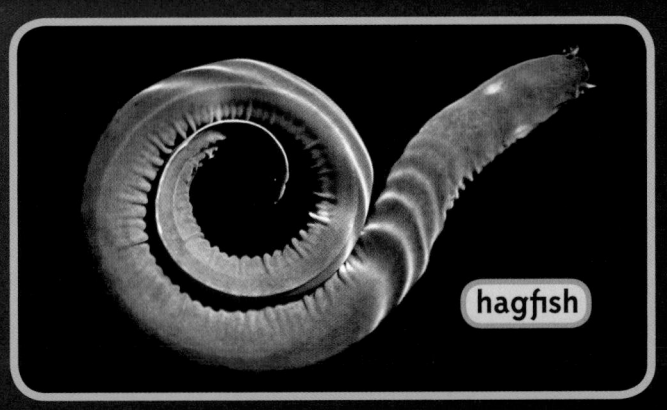
hagfish

A hagfish has a super strong sense of smell and touch. It can smell food that's fallen from higher up in the ocean. It also uses feelers to find meals.

Super Subs!

How do we know about weird sea creatures in the deep ocean?

People can't dive deep to see these strange creatures. It's too cold and dark there. And the water pressure is strong enough to crush a person.

But humans can use machines called submersibles (sub-MER-sih-bullz) to explore the deep ocean.

Sometimes people control them from far away, like a remote-controlled car. And sometimes people ride inside.

4,764 feet

How Deep?

This submersible, named Alvin, can dive 4,764 feet deep. It would take more than three Empire State Buildings stacked up to reach that depth.

These odd tube worms live on the bottom of the ocean. They can grow to be eight feet tall.

Submersibles collect information. They have lights and special tools. They take pictures, and they gather plants, rocks, and animals.

Scientists used submersibles to find the weird creatures shown here. And there are probably thousands more that have not been found yet.

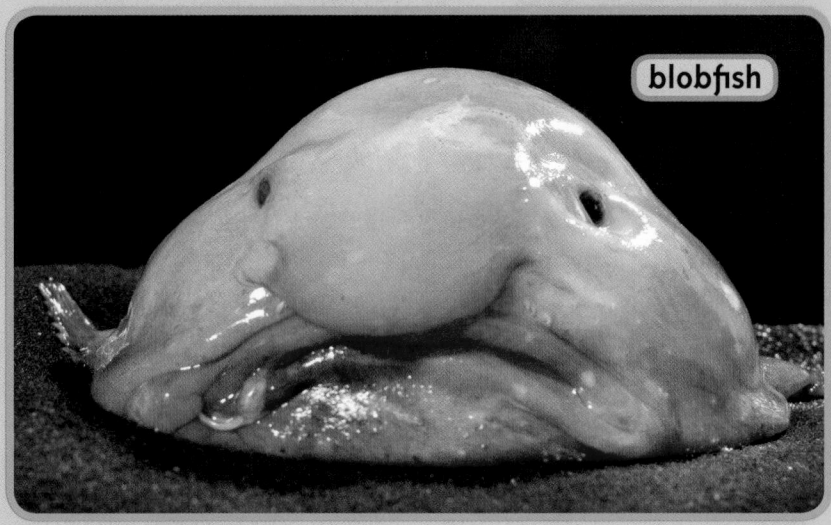

blobfish

Stump Your Parents

Can your parents answer these questions about sea creatures? You might know more than they do!

Answers are at the bottom of page 31.

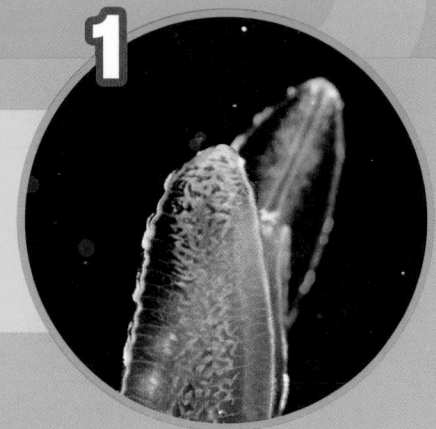

1

Bioluminescence is ____.
A. a loud sound
B. the light an animal makes
C. a search for food
D. a fast swim

2

Machines that dive deep in the ocean are called ____.
A. speedboats
B. planes
C. submersibles
D. scuba suits

3

Which features are common in deep-sea animals?
A. big mouth
B. big teeth
C. big eyes
D. all of the above

Animals that have venom are _____.

A. not harmful
B. friendly
C. able to cause stinging, pain, or death
D. only found in shallow waters

Humans can't scuba dive deep into the ocean because _____.

A. it's too cold
B. it's too dark
C. the pressure is too great
D. all of the above

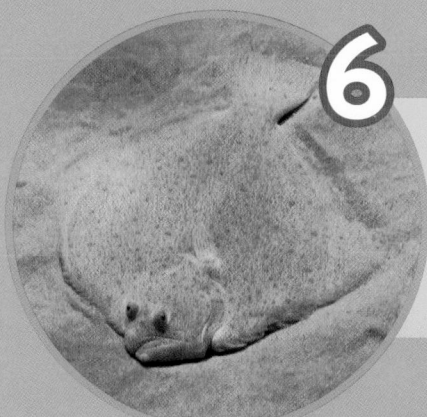

What is camouflage?

A. a way of eating
B. a way to blend in and hide
C. how animals see in the dark
D. none of the above

An animal that is eaten by another animal is called _____.

A. prey
B. an anemone
C. a tentacle
D. a creature

Answers: 1) B, 2) C, 3) D, 4) C, 5) D, 6) B, 7) A

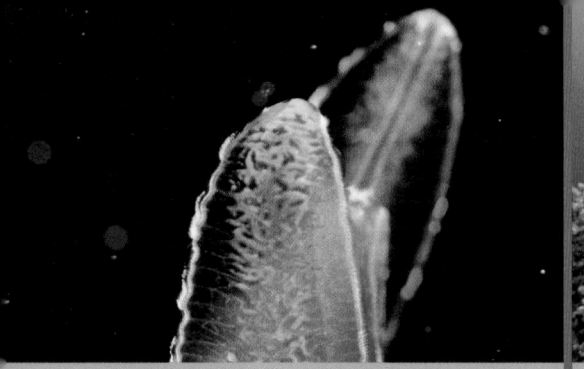

BIOLUMINESCENCE: Light that an animal makes by itself

CAMOUFLAGE: An animal's natural color or form that blends in with what is around it

PREDATOR: An animal that hunts and eats other animals

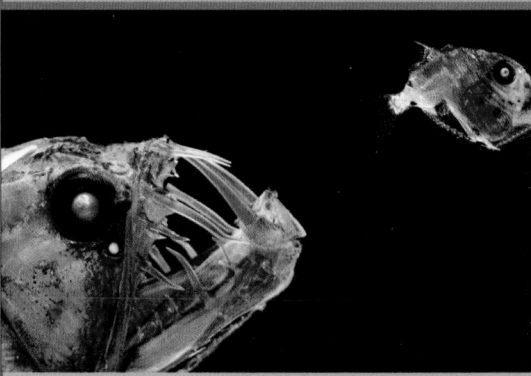

PREY: An animal that is eaten by another animal

SUBMERSIBLE: An underwater craft used to explore and gather information

VENOM: A liquid some animals make that can cause stinging, pain, or death